Celebrate the Seasons!

It's Winter!

By
Linda Glaser

Illustrated by
Susan Swan

The Millbrook Press
Brookfield, Connecticut

For my dear friend Marnie, who has
shared countless hikes and outdoor
adventures with me in all seasons.

LG

For Gabriel, Britney, Cody,
Ashley, Jordan, and
Madison, with wishes for
endless seasons of joy to come.

SS

Copyright © 2002 by Linda Glaser
Illustrations copyright © 2002 by Susan Swan

Library of Congress Cataloging-in-Publication Data
Glaser, Linda.
It's winter! / by Linda Glaser ; illustrated by
Susan Swan.
p. cm. – (Celebrate the seasons!)
Summary: A child observes the coming of winter
and its effects on the weather, animals, and plants.
Includes suggestions for wintertime activities.
ISBN 0-7613-1759-7 (lib. bdg.)
ISBN 0-7613-1680-9 (pbk.)
[1. Winter–Fiction.] I. Swan, Susan, ill.
II. Title. III. Series.
PZ7.G48047 Iv 2002   [E]–dc21   2001044771

Published by The Millbrook Press, Inc.
2 Old New Milford Road
Brookfield, Connecticut 06804
http://www.millbrookpress.com

Printed in Hong Kong
lib   5 4 3 2 1
pbk 5 4 3 2 1

It's
Winter!

I chase and zigzag
here
and
there,

catching snowflakes in the air.
They land on my face and on my hair.

I stick out my tongue
and catch one.
Yum!

Flakes and flakes
and flakes
float down
down
down.

Some melt, but some stick
when they touch the bare ground.
I can hardly wait
to wake up and see
how deep the snow
will finally be!

We're all bundled up in warm snowsuits
with scarves and hats and mittens and boots.
The snow's so bright we have to squint.
Each step we take we sink,

sink,

sink...

making **deep** footprints.

It's winter!
We make snow angels
and build a snowman and snow lady.
They sparkle brightly in the sun.
I don't even feel cold. I'm having so much fun.

Bare tree branches reach up high,
sketching brown tree patterns in the sky.
There's a tap, tap, tap.
I look up and see a woodpecker pecking at a tree.

My breath comes out
in small white puffs.
I trudge in my snow boots going squeak,
crunch, crunch.

The air's so cold it freezes the hairs inside my nose.

Brrrr!

One day I get a letter from my Grandma and Grandpa, who live down south in Florida. They say it's hot and sunny.

Oooh! That seems strange and funny. Our winters are so different. It's hard to believe. But see? Here's a photo of them sunning on the beach.

Meanwhile, here up north,
in caves where I can't see,
little brown bats are hibernating.
They don't eat or move. They barely breathe.
They all huddle together
and sleep, sleep, sleep.
Shhh.

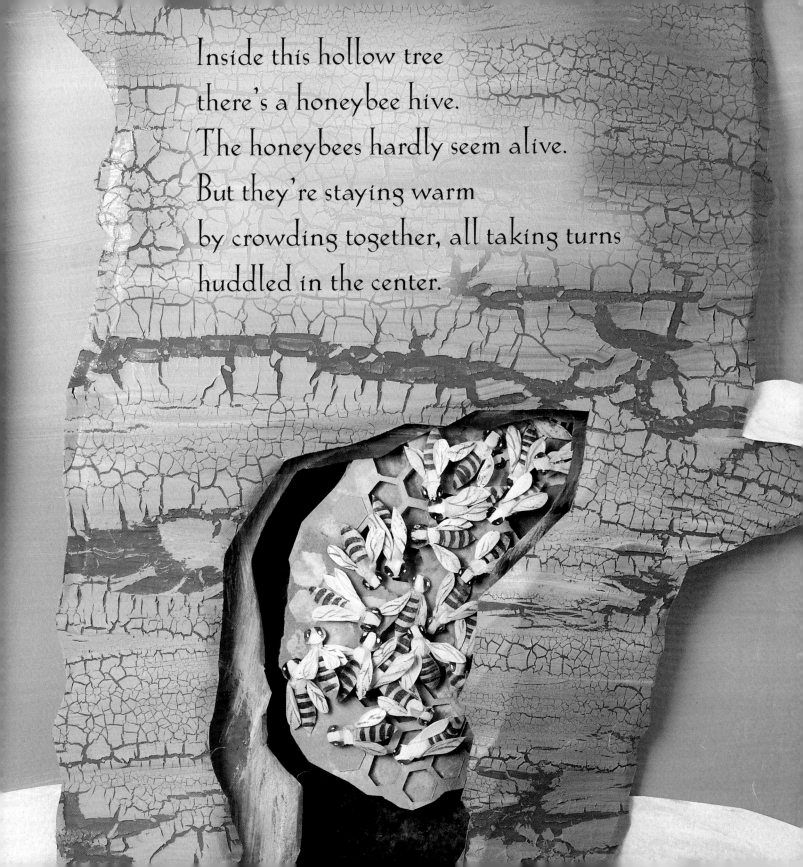

Inside this hollow tree
there's a honeybee hive.
The honeybees hardly seem alive.
But they're staying warm
by crowding together, all taking turns
huddled in the center.

It's winter!
Way, way down under my feet,
turtles, snakes, and earthworms are fast asleep.
Groundhogs are also curled in sleep.
Their hearts go so slowly. They barely beat.

Chipmunks sleep underground
on piles of nuts and seeds.
Sometimes they wake up,
take a quick snack, and then
go back to sleep. Shhh.

We skate around on the frozen pond.

And way under the ice,
down in the soft mud,
dragonfly nymphs are
fast asleep
and so are
hibernating frogs.

It's winter!
But even here up north, not all
the animals are asleep. Deer come
to eat the tender twigs
and bark of trees.
Gray squirrels leap from
branch to branch and tree to tree.
Whee!

Every day I scatter birdseed.
Then lots of birds swoop down to eat.
We get sparrows, cardinals, blue jays, and chickadees.
They eat and eat and cheep,
                              cheep,
                                    cheep.

The sun sets early. The days seem short.

Even before dinner, it's already dark.

We search the night sky for winter constellations.

Look up there! I see Orion.

The moon glows with a soft, creamy light.

And ooh! There's a halo around it tonight.

I spot a snowshoe hare—just sitting there.
Its white coat blends in with the snow.
But soon, in the spring, its fur will
turn brown to blend with the ground.

One day we notice that some snow is melting.
The sun feels stronger. The ground is getting warmer.
Soon, very soon, spring will be here.
But right now it's still winter.

We slide down smooth and slippery hills.
Wheee! Watch us go.

Oh, I hope we get another snow!
It's winter! It's winter!

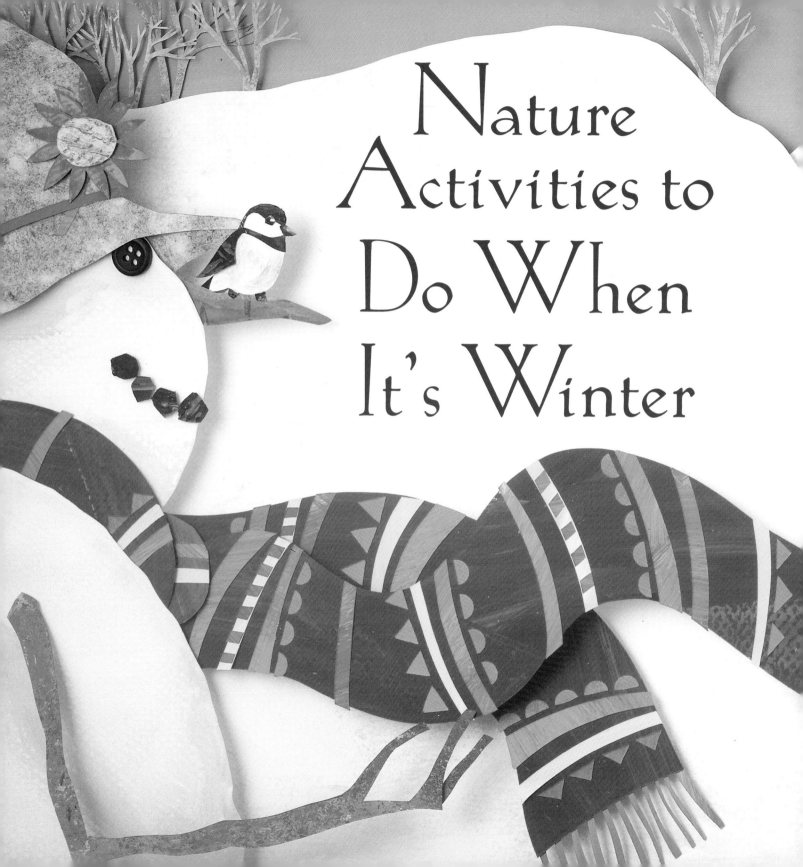

Nature
Activities to
Do When
It's Winter

Feed the winter birds. Scatter birdseed on the ground or fill a bird feeder. Once you start feeding winter birds, don't stop until well into spring. The birds are counting on you for their food.

Make an easy pinecone bird feeder. First tie a string around the top of a pinecone. Then spread peanut butter onto the pinecone. Roll the pinecone in birdseed. Hang your pinecone bird feeder from the branch of a tree.

Keep a bird list of all the different birds you see.

Dig under the snow and find green moss. Make sure to cover it up again. Under the snow it's warmer, and the moss is able to survive all winter.

Find as many different types of evergreen trees as you can. See if you can identify them.

Listen to winter sounds—the crack of ice, the crunch of snow on your snow boots, the calls of winter birds.

Notice animal tracks and try to identify them.

Go snow shoeing, sledding, ice-skating.

Make snow angels. Build a snow fort or a snow house. Make big snow animals that you can "ride."

Catch some snowflakes on dark paper or fabric and look at them under a magnifying glass.

Go to a frozen stream with a grown-up and notice the ice formations and the water running underneath. Make sure to stay on the ground—NOT on the ice.

Take a walk in the woods with a grown-up. If you're quiet, you may spot some winter birds or animals. But if you find any animals hibernating—like bats, butterflies, or ladybugs, leave them alone. If they are woken up, they may die.

See if you can spot a cocoon hanging from the branch of a tree or on the ground. It may look like a dead leaf, but when the weather gets warmer a moth will come out.

See if you can find pointy leaf buds on trees or bushes. Notice how they are tightly wrapped to stay warm all winter.

Fill a plastic pail with snow. Bring it inside and see how much water there is when it melts.

Collect some very clean fresh snow and make a snowball. Put it into a cone. Pour some maple syrup on it and eat your snow cone.

During the winter, not all places have snow and freezing temperatures. Check the Internet for other cities around the country and around the world to see what kind of weather they are having. Imagine what the children there are doing.

If you do live where there is snow, put a snowball into a plastic container and store it in the freezer. In the summer, take it out and hold it against your cheek and remember the winter.

About the Author and Illustrator

Linda Glaser is the author of many successful nonfiction picture books on natural history subjects. Her books SPECTACULAR SPIDERS, COMPOST!, WONDERFUL WORMS, and OUR BIG HOME: AN EARTH POEM were all named Outstanding Science Trade Books for Children by the Children's Book Council/National Science Teachers Association. In addition to teaching and writing, she conducts writing workshops for schoolchildren and for adults. She lives in Minnesota.

For IT'S WINTER!, Susan Swan created three-dimensional cut-paper artwork. First she selected her papers and then hand painted them to get the colors and textures she needed to achieve the palette of winter. She then cut and layered the papers to accomplish the dramatic sense of depth that gives life to each piece of art. Finally, Susan's husband, Terry, photographed the finished artwork with lighting that accents the shadows of the paper. Susan and her husband are, professionally, Swan & Rasberry Studios, and they live in Texas.